## THE CANADIAN LIVING
### COOKING
### COLLECTION

# SOUPS
# AND STARTERS

The following Canadian companies were involved in the production
of this Collection: Colour Technologies, Fred Bird & Associates Limited,
Gordon Sibley Design Inc., On-line Graphics, Telemedia Publishing Inc. and
The Madison Book Group Inc.

Canadian Living is a trademark of Telemedia Publishing Inc.
All trademark rights, registered and unregistered, are reserved.

We acknowledge the contribution of
Drew Warner, Joie Warner and Flavor Publications.

**Produced by**
**The Madison Book Group Inc.**
**40 Madison Avenue**
**Toronto, Ontario**
**Canada**
**M5R 2S1**

# SOUPS AND STARTERS

■ *On our cover:
Ranchero Meatball
Soup (p. 12)*

Soup is one of the most satisfying, versatile and easy-to-prepare dishes you can serve. And with the over 35 recipes we feature here, you'll find delicious soups that suit any meal you're planning. We've included hearty main-dish favorites like *Ranchero Meatball Soup, French Onion Soup* and *Savory Bean and Sausage Soup* that are perfect for lunches or quick weekday suppers — along with refreshing make-ahead starters like *Strawberry Soup, Cucumber Yogurt Soup* and *Buttermilk Soup in Pepper Shells*.

We've rounded out this book with an assortment of easy appetizers like *Multilayered Mexican Dip, Stuffed Jumbo Shrimp* and *Red Pepper Bruschetta* that are just as delicious for family snacking as they are for casual entertaining.

**Soups and Starters** is just one of the eight full-color cookbooks that make up THE CANADIAN LIVING COOKING COLLECTION. Inside each of these colorful cookbooks are the kind of satisfying, easy-to-make dishes you'll want to cook over and over again. Each recipe in the Collection has been carefully selected and tested by *Canadian Living* to make sure it turns out wonderfully every time you make it. When you collect all eight cookbooks, you can choose from over 500 dishes — from marvelous soups to sensational desserts — all guaranteed to make any meal extra special.

*Elizabeth Baird*

**Elizabeth Baird**
**Food Director,** *Canadian Living* **Magazine**

# Savory Bean and Sausage Soup

*Instead of the quick-soaking method for beans, you can also combine them with water and let stand for 8 hours or overnight, then drain, discarding water, rinse and drain again.*

| | | |
|---|---|---|
| 2 cups | Great Northern beans (1 lb/500 g) | 500 mL |
| 1/4 lb | slab bacon | 125 g |
| 3 tbsp | olive oil | 50 mL |
| 2 | large onions, chopped | 2 |
| 3 | cloves garlic, minced | 3 |
| 1 | stalk celery, chopped | 1 |
| 1 | carrot, diced | 1 |
| 6 cups | water | 1.5 L |
| 2 | bay leaves | 2 |
| 1-1/2 tsp | paprika | 7 mL |
| 1/2 tsp | ground coriander | 2 mL |
| 1/2 tsp | dried thyme | 2 mL |
| 1/4 tsp | dried marjoram | 1 mL |
| Pinch | saffron | Pinch |
| 1 | can (14 oz/398 mL) tomatoes | 1 |
| 1/4 lb | prosciutto ham (in 1 piece) | 125 g |
| 1/2 lb | dried chorizo sausage or pepperoni | 250 g |
| | Salt and pepper | |
| 1/2 cup | chopped fresh parsley | 125 mL |
| | Garlic croutons (recipe follows) | |

■ To quick-soak beans, cover with 3 times their volume of cold water; bring to boil and boil gently for 2 minutes. Remove from heat; cover and let stand for 1 hour. Drain, discarding water; rinse and drain again.

■ Dice bacon into 1/2-inch (1 cm) pieces. In large Dutch oven or saucepan, heat oil over medium-high heat; cook bacon, stirring, until lightly golden, 5 to 7 minutes. With slotted spoon, transfer to bowl.

■ Discard all but 3 tbsp (50 mL) fat; cook onions, garlic, celery and carrot for 5 to 7 minutes or until softened. Add bacon, beans, water, bay leaves, paprika, coriander, thyme, marjoram and saffron; bring to boil. Reduce heat to medium-low; cover and simmer until beans are tender, about 1 hour.

■ Chop tomatoes into bite-size pieces; add to soup. Finely dice prosciutto and thinly slice chorizo; add to soup. Simmer, uncovered, for 10 minutes or until heated through. Remove bay leaves. Season with salt and pepper to taste. Sprinkle parsley and Garlic Croutons on each serving. Makes 6 servings.

### GARLIC CROUTONS

| | | |
|---|---|---|
| 5 | slices bread | 5 |
| 1 tbsp | olive oil | 15 mL |
| 3 | cloves garlic, minced | 3 |

■ Trim crusts from bread. Cut slices into 1/2-inch (1 cm) cubes. In skillet, heat oil over medium heat; cook garlic and bread cubes, stirring often, for 3 to 5 minutes or until croutons are crisp and golden. Drain on paper towels.

# Potato and Squash Soup with Walnut-Gruyère Toast

*Serve this hearty soup in shallow old-fashioned bowls and float a slice of grilled Walnut-Gruyère Toast on top of each portion.*

| | | |
|---|---|---|
| 2 tbsp | butter | 25 mL |
| 1 cup | finely chopped onions | 250 mL |
| 3 cups | diced peeled potatoes | 750 mL |
| 3 cups | diced peeled butternut squash | 750 mL |
| 4 cups | chicken stock | 1 L |
| 1 cup | finely shredded spinach | 250 mL |
| 1/4 cup | finely sliced green onions (green part only) | 50 mL |
| 3/4 tsp | cider vinegar | 4 mL |
| | Salt and pepper | |
| | **WALNUT-GRUYÈRE TOAST** | |
| 6 | slices Italian or French bread | 6 |
| 2 cups | shredded Gruyère cheese (6 oz/175 g) | 500 mL |
| 1/3 cup | freshly grated Parmesan cheese | 75 mL |
| 1/4 cup | finely chopped walnuts | 50 mL |
| 6 | walnut halves (optional) | 6 |

■ In large heavy saucepan, melt butter over low heat; cover and cook onions for 3 to 5 minutes or until softened. Stir in potatoes and squash, coating evenly.

■ Pour in stock; cover and bring to boil over high heat. Reduce heat and simmer for about 30 minutes or until vegetables are tender. Remove from heat. Mash vegetables lightly to thicken soup but do not purée. Stir in spinach, green onions, vinegar, and salt and pepper to taste.

■ **Walnut-Gruyère Toast:** Meanwhile, broil bread on one side about 4 inches (10 cm) from heat until toasted. Turn and sprinkle with Gruyère, Parmesan and chopped walnuts; broil until cheese is bubbly and nuts are toasted.

■ Ladle soup into bowls. Float 1 toast on each; garnish with walnut half (if using). Makes 6 servings.

# Yellow Pepper Soup with Red Pepper Purée

*This soup is easy to prepare and very pretty. If you purée the soup in a food mill, don't peel the yellow peppers because the food mill will strain out the skins. To peel the yellow peppers and roast the red pepper for the purée, see Roasted Peppers, opposite page.*

| | | |
|---|---|---|
| 2 tbsp | butter | 25 mL |
| 1 | onion, chopped | 1 |
| 1 | clove garlic, minced | 1 |
| 4 | sweet yellow peppers, peeled and diced | 4 |
| 2 tbsp | all-purpose flour | 25 mL |
| 2 cups | chicken stock | 500 mL |
| 1/2 cup | whipping cream (optional) | 125 mL |
| | Salt and pepper | |
| | Red Pepper Purée (recipe follows) | |
| | Fresh basil sprigs | |

■ In saucepan, melt butter over medium heat; cook onion and garlic for 3 to 4 minutes or until tender but not browned. Add yellow peppers; cook for 5 to 8 minutes or until fragrant and wilted. Stir in flour and cook, without browning, for 4 minutes.

■ Add chicken stock; bring to boil. Reduce heat and simmer gently for 20 minutes. In food processor or blender, purée yellow pepper mixture until smooth. *(Recipe can be prepared to this point, covered and refrigerated for up to 2 days.)*

■ Return yellow pepper mixture to saucepan; add cream (if using) and cook just until heated through but do not boil. Season soup with salt and pepper to taste.

■ Ladle soup into wide shallow dishes. Swirl dollops of Red Pepper Purée through soup. Garnish with basil. Makes 4 to 6 servings.

### RED PEPPER PURÉE

| | | |
|---|---|---|
| 1 | sweet red pepper, roasted and peeled | 1 |
| 1 | clove garlic, minced | 1 |
| 1/4 tsp | salt | 1 mL |
| 1/4 tsp | hot pepper sauce | 1 mL |

■ In food processor or blender, process red pepper, garlic, salt and hot pepper sauce until smooth. Transfer to small bowl. *(Purée can be covered and refrigerated for up to 2 days. Bring to room temperature before swirling into soup.)* Makes about 1/2 cup (125 mL).

# Sausage and Leek Soup

*Double this recipe if you wish, and freeze half for future meals.*

| | | |
|---|---|---|
| 1/4 cup | butter | 50 mL |
| 2 cups | sliced leeks (white part only) | 500 mL |
| 3/4 cup | diced carrots | 175 mL |
| 3/4 cup | diced celery | 175 mL |
| 2 tbsp | all-purpose flour | 25 mL |
| 4 cups | chicken stock | 1 L |
| 2 cups | diced peeled potatoes | 500 mL |
| 1/4 lb | Polish sausage, thinly sliced | 125 g |
| 1/2 tsp | salt | 2 mL |
| 1/4 tsp | dried marjoram | 1 mL |
| | Pepper | |

■ In large saucepan, melt butter over medium heat; cook leeks, carrots and celery until softened but not browned. Add flour and cook for 2 minutes, stirring constantly.

■ Blend in chicken stock. Add potatoes and bring to boil. Reduce heat and simmer for 15 minutes until vegetables are tender. Add sausage, salt, marjoram, and pepper to taste; simmer for 10 minutes. Makes 6 servings.

---

## ROASTED PEPPERS

*If you want to enjoy roasted peppers all year round, but hate paying out-of-season prices, here are several ways to roast them for freezing. For a deep roast flavor, the best way is to broil or grill them on the barbecue. If the peppers you're grilling are hot, such as cayenne, jalapeño and banana, be sure to wear rubber gloves and avoid touching any part of your body with them.*

*• Grill peppers for about 15 minutes, turning with tongs as each side browns and puffs. Let cool, peel and remove seeds, reserving any juices.*

*• Broil peppers 4 inches (10 cm) from heat following directions for grilling.*

*• Roast sweet red or yellow peppers only in shallow roasting pan in 375°F (190°C) oven for about 30 minutes, turning once, or until puffed and lightly browned. Let cool, peel and remove seeds, reserving any juices.*

*• Freeze convenient amounts of peppers and juices in freezer bags or containers.*

# *Tomato Soup with Pesto*

*This soup is a striking contrast of colors and flavors. If making pesto ahead of time, cover it with a thin layer of olive oil to prevent discoloration and refrigerate for up to one week.*

| | | | | | |
|---|---|---|---|---|---|
| 2 tbsp | olive oil | 25 mL | | **PESTO** | |
| 1/3 cup | chopped shallots | 75 mL | 1 cup | fresh basil | 250 mL |
| 8 cups | chopped seeded peeled tomatoes | 2 L | 1/4 cup | freshly grated Parmesan cheese (or 2 tbsp/25 mL each Parmesan and Romano) | 50 mL |
| 2 tsp | salt | 10 mL | | | |
| | Pepper | | 1/4 cup | olive oil | 50 mL |
| | Pesto (recipe follows) | | 1 | clove garlic | 1 |
| | | | 1 tbsp | pine nuts or chopped walnuts | 15 mL |
| | | | 1/4 tsp | salt | 1 mL |

■ In large saucepan, heat oil over medium heat; sauté shallots until softened but not browned. Add tomatoes, salt, and pepper to taste. Reduce heat to low, cover and simmer for 10 minutes. Transfer to food processor; purée until smooth. Ladle into soup bowls; swirl 1 tbsp (15 mL) Pesto into each bowl. Makes 6 to 8 servings.

■ In food processor or blender, combine basil, cheese, oil, garlic, nuts and salt; process until finely chopped but not too smooth, scraping down sides once or twice. Add 1 to 2 tbsp (15 to 25 mL) hot water to thin sauce to cake batter consistency. Makes about 1/2 cup (125 mL).

# Ranchero Meatball Soup

*If you like chili, you'll love this soup. Accompany with a green salad and tortilla chips. You can substitute black beans for the kidney beans as we did for our photograph.*

| | | |
|---|---|---|
| 4 cups | beef stock | 1 L |
| 1 | can (19 oz/540 mL) tomatoes (undrained) | 1 |
| 2 | small onions, chopped | 2 |
| 1 | clove garlic, minced | 1 |
| 1 tsp | chili powder | 5 mL |
| 1/2 tsp | cumin | 2 mL |
| 1/3 cup | long-grain rice | 75 mL |
| 1 | egg | 1 |
| 1 tsp | dried oregano | 5 mL |
| 1/2 tsp | salt | 2 mL |
| 1 lb | ground beef | 500 g |
| 1 | can (19 oz/540 mL) kidney beans (undrained) | 1 |
| Half | sweet green or/and yellow pepper, coarsely chopped | Half |
| 1 | small zucchini, sliced | 1 |

■ In large saucepan, stir together stock, tomatoes, 1 of the onions, garlic, chili powder and cumin; bring to boil. Reduce heat and simmer, covered, for about 30 minutes or until flavors have blended.

■ Meanwhile, in small bowl, soak rice in enough hot water to cover for 15 minutes.

■ In large bowl, beat together egg, remaining onion, oregano and salt; mix in beef, breaking up with spoon. Drain rice; stir into beef mixture to make moist mixture. With moistened hands, shape into 1-inch (2.5 cm) balls.

■ Add meatballs and beans to saucepan; bring to boil. Reduce heat, cover and simmer for 15 minutes. Add green pepper and zucchini; cover and simmer for about 10 minutes or until meatballs are no longer pink inside. Taste and adjust seasoning if necessary. Makes about 4 servings.

---

*MAKING MEATBALLS*
*Use a measuring spoon to help keep meatballs the same size. As a general measure, 1-1/2 tsp (7 mL) makes a 1-inch (2.5 cm) ball; 4 tsp (20 mL) makes a 1-1/2-inch (4 cm) ball. Or roll mixture into a cylinder, cut into equal slices and form into meatballs.*

---

# Red Cabbage Borscht

*A distant but delicious relative to true borscht, this variation has beautiful color and is easy to make in winter with canned beets.*

| | | |
|---|---|---|
| 1 | can (14 oz/398 mL) whole beets | 1 |
| 2 tbsp | butter | 25 mL |
| 1 | large onion, finely chopped | 1 |
| 1 | clove garlic, minced | 1 |
| 1-1/2 cups | shredded red cabbage | 375 mL |
| 1 | can (19 oz/540 mL) tomatoes | 1 |
| 2 cups | water | 500 mL |
| 1/4 cup | red wine vinegar | 50 mL |
| 1 | can (10 oz/284 mL) beef stock | 1 |
| 1 tsp | granulated sugar | 5 mL |
| 1 tsp | dried dillweed | 5 mL |
| 1 tsp | caraway seeds (optional) | 5 mL |
| | Salt and pepper | |
| | Sour cream (optional) | |

■ Drain beets and reserve liquid; chop beets.
■ In large heavy saucepan, melt butter; cook onion until softened. Add garlic and cabbage; cook, stirring, until cabbage is wilted. Add beets and reserved liquid, tomatoes, water, vinegar, stock, sugar, dillweed and caraway seeds (if using).

■ Cover and simmer for about 30 minutes or until cabbage is very soft. Season with salt and pepper to taste. If desired, purée until almost smooth in food processor or blender. Serve very hot; garnish each serving with dollop of sour cream (if using). Makes about 6 servings.

*SOUP-ER HINTS*
*Simmer soups (keeping the broth just below the boiling point) rather than boil them. Meat and vegetables will be more tender; broth will be clearer.*
*• The smaller the pieces of meat and vegetables, the faster the soups will cook.*
*• Most main-course soups will keep for five days in the refrigerator and can also be frozen successfully.*
*• Reheating brings out the flavor of salt, pepper and other seasonings — so go easy on the seasonings the first time around.*

# Pumpkin Soup

*Pumpkin or squash soups are delightful served in a hollowed-out squash or pumpkin shell. From this basic recipe, you can also prepare a delicate velvety cream soup flavored with orange and a more rustic version enlivened with a little hot pepper and crunchy garnish.*

| | | |
|---|---|---|
| 1/4 cup | butter | 50 mL |
| 1 | large onion, chopped | 1 |
| 2 | leeks, chopped (white parts only) | 2 |
| 1 | large potato, peeled and diced | 1 |
| 1 cup | pumpkin purée or 3 cups (750 mL) diced raw pumpkin | 250 mL |
| 3 cups | chicken stock | 750 mL |
| 1-1/2 cups | (approx) light cream | 375 mL |
| Pinch | each nutmeg and cayenne pepper | Pinch |
| | Salt and pepper | |
| Pinch | basil (optional) | Pinch |
| | **GARNISH** | |
| | Chopped chives, green onion or fresh basil | |

■ In large heavy saucepan, melt butter; cook onion and leeks until softened but not browned. Add potato and pumpkin; stir in chicken stock. Bring to boil; reduce heat and simmer, covered, until all vegetables are softened, about 20 minutes.

■ In food processor or blender, process mixture until desired smoothness. Return to saucepan. Add enough of the cream to reach desired consistency; gradually heat until very hot but do not boil. Add nutmeg, cayenne pepper, and basil (if using). Season with salt and pepper to taste. Sprinkle each serving with chives. Makes 4 to 6 servings.

VARIATIONS

**Orange Pumpkin Soup:** Add 1/2 cup (125 mL) frozen orange juice concentrate along with chicken stock. Garnish with chives and orange slices.

**Peppery Pumpkin Soup:** Add 1 clove garlic, minced, to onion and leeks. Add dash hot pepper sauce along with cayenne, or add small piece of hot chili pepper during cooking. Substitute dried thyme for nutmeg. Garnish with lightly sautéed toasted pumpkin seeds or pine nuts.

# Cream of Leek Soup

*This creamy, smooth soup is wonderful hot, cold or warm. Grated carrot or puréed squash may be added if desired.*

| 1/4 cup | butter | 50 mL |
|---|---|---|
| 6 | large leeks, chopped (white part only) | 6 |
| 1 | small onion, chopped | 1 |
| 5 cups | chicken stock | 1.25 L |
| 2 cups | diced peeled potatoes (about 2 large) | 500 mL |
| 1/4 tsp | white pepper | 1 mL |
| | Salt | |
| 1 cup | light cream | 250 mL |
| 1/4 cup | white wine | 50 mL |
| | Chopped chives | |

■ In large heavy saucepan, melt butter; gently cook leeks and onion until softened but not browned, about 20 minutes. Add chicken stock and potatoes; cook for 20 to 30 minutes or until potatoes are tender. Add pepper, and salt to taste.

■ In food processor or blender, purée soup until smooth. Return to saucepan; heat to boiling. Add cream and wine; heat through but do not boil. Taste and adjust seasoning if necessary. Ladle into bowls; sprinkle with chives. Makes 6 to 8 servings.

---

*FLAVORINGS FOR SOUPS*
*Experiment with flavorings to subtly alter the taste of soups.*
*For clear soups:*
• *Splash of brandy, sherry, white or red wine*
• *Freshly grated gingerroot or nutmeg*
• *Freshly squeezed lemon or lime juice*
• *White or red wine vinegar*
*For cream soups:*
• *Fresh or dried herbs: marjoram, thyme or oregano*
• *Spices: Toasted ground cumin or coriander seeds*
*For fruit soups:*
• *Fruit liqueur or eau-de-vie*

# *Minestrone*

*Chock-full of vegetables, beans and pasta, minestrone is handy to have around on those nights when everyone is on the run and eating at various times. This soup is light because the vegetables aren't sautéed in oil.*

| | | |
|---|---|---|
| 1/2 lb | lean ground beef | 250 g |
| 1 | large onion, diced | 1 |
| 1 | carrot, diced | 1 |
| 1 | stalk celery, diced | 1 |
| 1 | small zucchini, diced | 1 |
| 1 | can (14 oz/398 mL) tomatoes (undrained), chopped | 1 |
| 1 | potato, peeled and diced | 1 |
| 3 | cloves garlic, diced | 3 |
| 6 cups | water or chicken stock | 1.5 L |
| 3/4 cup | small pasta | 175 mL |
| 1 tsp | each dried oregano and basil | 5 mL |
| 1 | can (19 oz/540 mL) white kidney beans, drained | 1 |
| 1/2 cup | chopped fresh parsley | 125 mL |
| 1/3 cup | freshly grated Parmesan cheese | 75 mL |
| Dash | hot pepper sauce | Dash |
| | Salt and pepper | |

■ In large saucepan, cook meat over medium heat until browned, breaking up with fork; drain off fat. Add onion; cook, stirring, for 3 minutes.

■ Add carrot, celery, zucchini, tomatoes, potato and garlic; cook, stirring, for 3 minutes. Add water; bring to boil. Add pasta, oregano and basil; cook for 10 to 12 minutes or until pasta is tender but firm and vegetables are cooked. Add kidney beans, parsley, Parmesan cheese and hot pepper sauce; heat through. Season with salt and pepper to taste. Makes 8 servings.

# Potato and Carrot Soup

*Chilled potato soup is popular at everything from picnics to special dinner parties. Carrots can give it a bright new look.*

| | | |
|---|---|---|
| 2 tbsp | butter | 25 mL |
| 2 | small leeks or 1 large, chopped (white part only) | 2 |
| 1 | large onion, chopped | 1 |
| 1 tsp | dried thyme | 5 mL |
| 3 | potatoes, peeled and diced | 3 |
| 2 | large carrots, sliced | 2 |
| 4 cups | chicken stock | 1 L |
| 1-1/2 cups | (approx) light cream | 375 mL |
| | Salt and pepper | |
| | Chopped fresh mint | |

■ In saucepan, melt butter over medium heat; cook leeks, onion and thyme for about 5 minutes or until leeks and onion are softened. Stir in potatoes and carrots; cook for 3 minutes. Stir in stock; cover and simmer until vegetables are very tender, about 30 minutes.

■ In blender or food processor, purée soup in batches until smooth; transfer to bowl. Gradually whisk in cream, adding up to 1/2 cup (125 mL) more to reach desired consistency. Season with salt and pepper to taste. Cover and refrigerate for at least 4 hours or until chilled. Taste and adjust seasoning if necessary. Garnish each serving with mint. Makes 6 servings.

# Rich Creamed Mushroom Soup

*A bowl of this soothing, tasty soup adds comfort to any cold winter's day.*

| | | |
|---|---|---|
| 1/4 cup | butter | 50 mL |
| 1/2 cup | finely chopped onion | 125 mL |
| 1 | clove garlic, finely chopped | 1 |
| 2-1/2 cups | sliced fresh mushrooms | 625 mL |
| 1/4 cup | all-purpose flour | 50 mL |
| 4-1/2 cups | chicken stock | 1.12 L |
| 1 | small bay leaf | 1 |
| 1/2 tsp | salt | 2 mL |
| 1/4 tsp | pepper | 1 mL |
| 1 cup | light cream | 250 mL |
| 3 tbsp | finely chopped chives | 50 mL |

■ In large heavy saucepan, melt butter over medium heat; cook onion and garlic until onions are translucent, 3 to 4 minutes. Add mushrooms and stir well; cook for 3 minutes. Stir in flour to coat vegetables; cook, stirring, for 2 minutes.

■ Gradually stir in stock; add bay leaf, salt and pepper. Bring to boil; reduce heat and simmer for 15 minutes. Remove bay leaf. Stir in cream and heat through but do not boil. Taste and adjust seasoning if necessary. Garnish with chives. Makes 6 servings.

# Chicken Minestrone

*This hearty main-course soup will conquer wintery chills. Since the recipe makes such a large amount, you may want to freeze containers of it. Post a note on the containers to add stock or water when reheating since the soup becomes quite thick when cooled.*

| | | |
|---|---|---|
| 1 | stewing chicken (5 lb/2.2 kg) | 1 |
| | Bouquet garni* | |
| 1 tsp | salt | 5 mL |
| 1/2 cup | pearl barley | 125 mL |
| 1 cup | drained canned tomatoes | 250 mL |
| 1 tsp | dried basil | 5 mL |
| | Salt and pepper | |
| 2 tbsp | olive or vegetable oil | 25 mL |
| 4 | carrots, thinly sliced | 4 |
| 2 | small zucchini, diced | 2 |
| 1 | large onion, chopped | 1 |
| 2 | stalks celery, thinly sliced | 2 |
| 2 | cloves garlic, minced | 2 |
| 1 cup | small macaroni | 250 mL |
| 4 cups | lightly packed torn fresh spinach | 1 L |
| 1/4 cup | chopped fresh parsley | 50 mL |
| | Freshly grated Parmesan cheese | |

■ In large saucepan or stock pot, cover chicken, including any giblets except liver, with 16 to 20 cups (4 to 5 L) cold water. Bring to boil, skimming off any foam. Add bouquet garni and salt. Reduce heat, partially cover and simmer for about 2-1/2 hours or until thigh is fork-tender.

■ Remove chicken and set aside to cool slightly. Discard bouquet garni. Strain stock; remove fat. Bring stock to boil. Add barley and tomatoes, breaking up with fork. Add basil, and salt and pepper to taste. Reduce heat, cover and simmer for 10 minutes.

■ Meanwhile, in large skillet, heat oil over medium heat; cook carrots, zucchini, onion, celery and garlic for about 5 minutes or until softened. Add to stock; cover and simmer for 15 minutes. Add macaroni; simmer, uncovered, until tender but firm, about 5 minutes.

■ Meanwhile, remove skin and bones from chicken. Cut meat into bite-size pieces; add to soup along with spinach and parsley. Heat through; taste and adjust seasoning. *(Soup can be frozen for up to 4 months.)* Serve in warm bowls with sprinkling of cheese. Makes 8 to 10 servings.

*To make bouquet garni, cut stalk of celery in half. Place 1/2 tsp (2 mL) dried thyme, bay leaf and parsley sprig in curved part; tie remaining stalk on top, curved part down.

# Egg Drop Soup

*This is a colorful soup that's quick and easy to make.*

| | | |
|---|---|---|
| 4 cups | chicken stock | 1 L |
| 1/2 tsp | soy sauce | 2 mL |
| 1/2 cup | chopped cooked chicken | 125 mL |
| 1/2 cup | frozen green peas | 125 mL |
| 1/4 cup | thinly sliced green onion | 50 mL |
| 1 | egg, lightly beaten | 1 |

■ In saucepan, bring stock and soy sauce to boil. Add chicken, peas and onion; return to boil. Remove from heat; drizzle in egg in slow steady stream. Allow egg to set for 1 minute; stir gently before ladling into bowls. Makes 4 servings.

# Lentil Soup with Beef and Barley

*This soup is thick and flavorful, so it can be extended with more stock, water or tomato juice. The soup freezes and reheats well. Serve it with brown bread or biscuits and a salad.*

| | | |
|---|---|---|
| 1/2 lb | ground beef | 250 g |
| 6 cups | (approx) water or vegetable stock | 1.5 L |
| 1 cup | split lentils | 250 mL |
| 1/4 cup | barley | 50 mL |
| 1 | can (10 oz/284 mL) beef broth | 1 |
| 1 | large onion, chopped | 1 |
| 1 | clove garlic, minced | 1 |
| 1 | large carrot, diced | 1 |
| 1 | large stalk celery, diced | 1 |
| 2 cups | chopped canned or stewed tomatoes | 500 mL |
| 1 | small bay leaf | 1 |

| | | |
|---|---|---|
| Pinch | each dried thyme and basil | Pinch |
| | Salt and pepper | |
| | Chopped fresh parsley | |

■ In large heavy stock pot, brown beef lightly, stirring to break up; drain off fat. Add water, lentils, barley and beef broth; bring to boil. Reduce heat and simmer, covered, until lentils and barley are nearly tender, about 30 minutes.

■ Add onion, garlic, carrot, celery, tomatoes, bay leaf, thyme and basil; simmer for 1-1/2 hours. Remove bay leaf. Season with salt and pepper to taste. Serve sprinkled with parsley. Makes about 12 servings.

# Chinese Noodle Soup

*Fill up on this complete meal in one bowl. A few slivered red peppers add color, and a dash of sesame oil just before serving adds a nutty flavor.*

| | | |
|---|---|---|
| 1 tsp | vegetable oil | 5 mL |
| 1 | clove garlic, minced | 1 |
| 1 tsp | ginger | 5 mL |
| 8 cups | chicken stock | 2 L |
| 1/4 lb | capellini or angel hair pasta | 125 g |
| 2 | boneless skinless chicken breasts, thinly sliced | 2 |
| 1 | can (10 oz/284 mL) water chestnuts, drained and sliced | 1 |
| 2 cups | bean sprouts (1/4 lb/125 g) | 500 mL |
| 1 | pkg (10 oz/284 g) fresh spinach | 1 |
| | Salt and pepper | |
| 4 | green onions, sliced | 4 |

■ In Dutch oven or large saucepan, heat oil over medium-high heat; cook garlic and ginger, stirring, for 30 seconds or until fragrant. Pour in chicken stock; bring to boil, skimming off any foam.

■ Break capellini into thirds and add to pan; cook for 2 to 3 minutes or until pasta is tender but firm. Stir in chicken; cook for 1 minute. Add water chestnuts, bean sprouts and spinach; cook for 1 minute or until chicken is no longer pink inside. Season with salt and pepper to taste. Ladle into bowls; garnish with onions. Makes 4 servings.

*STOCK, BROTH, BOUILLON OR CONSOMMÉ*

*In recipes calling for chicken or beef stock, you can use homemade or canned stock, or stock prepared from purchased cubes or powdered bases. (Watch the seasoning in your recipe because some cubes and powdered bases are very salty.)*

*• Stock, broth and bouillon are basically the same — the clear liquid produced when meat, bones and vegetables are simmered in water to extract flavor and then strained. Stock can be made from meat, poultry, fish or vegetables. Stock is the base for many soups and sauces; it adds much more flavor than plain water.*

*• Consommé is stronger than bouillon; it is stock enriched with more meat and vegetables, concentrated and clarified.*

# Herbed Cream of Broccoli Soup

*This is quite a rich soup and can be served as a main course. If you offer it as a first course, keep the portions small.*

| | | |
|---|---|---|
| 2 tbsp | butter | 25 mL |
| 1/4 cup | chopped green onion | 50 mL |
| 2 tbsp | chopped fresh parsley | 25 mL |
| 4 cups | coarsely chopped broccoli | 1 L |
| 2 cups | chicken stock | 500 mL |
| 2 tbsp | chopped fresh dill | 25 mL |
| 1-1/2 tsp | fresh summer savory (or 1/2 tsp/2 mL dried) | 7 mL |
| 8 | small broccoli florets | 8 |
| 1 cup | light cream | 250 mL |
| 1/2 cup | milk | 125 mL |
| | Salt and pepper | |

■ In saucepan, melt butter over medium-low heat; cook onion and parsley, covered and stirring occasionally, until onion is tender.

■ Add chopped broccoli, stock, dill and savory; bring to simmer and cook, uncovered, for 20 minutes. Add florets; cook for 5 minutes longer. Remove florets with slotted spoon and reserve.

■ In food processor or blender, purée mixture until smooth; return to saucepan. Season with salt and pepper to taste. Combine cream and milk; add to purée and cook over medium-low heat just until heated through but not boiling. Add florets. Makes 4 to 6 servings.

# Rich Chicken Stock

*This is an invaluable ingredient to keep on hand in the refrigerator or freezer for making soups, sauces and gravies. Use the chicken pieces for sandwiches, soups, stews and casseroles.*

| | | |
|---|---|---|
| 1 | chicken (3 lb/1.5 kg), cut in pieces | 1 |
| 6 cups | (approx) water | 1.5 L |
| 1 | slice gingerroot | 1 |
| 1 tsp | salt | 5 mL |
| 2 | green onions, chopped | 2 |

■ In large stock pot, combine chicken, water, gingerroot, salt and onions; bring to boil. Reduce heat and simmer, uncovered, for 1-1/2 hours, skimming off foam occasionally and adding water if necessary to keep chicken covered.

■ Let cool to lukewarm; remove chicken and reserve for another use.

■ Strain stock and refrigerate until chilled and fat congeals on surface. Remove fat. Makes about 6 cups (1.5 L).

# Chunky Tomato Gazpacho

*Here's an easy alternative to gazpacho that can be made in minutes. It's wonderful with French bread or sandwiches.*

| | | |
|---|---|---|
| 6 | tomatoes, peeled, seeded and chopped | 6 |
| 1 cup | chopped seeded cucumber or sweet green pepper | 250 mL |
| 4 | green onions, chopped | 4 |
| 2 tbsp | chopped fresh basil or parsley | 25 mL |
| 2 cups | chilled tomato juice | 500 mL |
| 1/4 cup | olive oil | 50 mL |
| | Salt and pepper | |

■ In large glass bowl, combine tomatoes, cucumber, green onions and basil; stir in tomato juice and oil. Season with salt and pepper to taste. Refrigerate until chilled. Makes 6 servings.

# Creamed Carrot Soup

*Full of satisfying flavor, this soup is both easy to prepare and attractive to present.*

| | | |
|---|---|---:|
| 2 tbsp | butter | 25 mL |
| 1 | onion, finely chopped | 1 |
| 6 | medium or 9 small carrots, diced | 6 |
| 1/4 cup | all-purpose flour | 50 mL |
| 6 cups | chicken stock | 1.5 L |
| 1 | bay leaf | 1 |
| 1/2 tsp | granulated sugar | 2 mL |
| 1/4 tsp | dried thyme | 1 mL |
| 2 | sprigs fresh parsley | 2 |
| 1 cup | milk | 250 mL |
| 1/2 cup | whipping cream | 125 mL |
| 3 tbsp | each finely chopped fresh parsley and chives | 50 mL |
| | Salt | |

■ In large heavy saucepan, melt butter over low heat; cook onion, covered, for 1 minute. Add carrots and stir to coat; cover and cook for 15 minutes, stirring occasionally.

■ Stir in flour; cook, stirring, for 2 minutes. Gradually stir in stock; add bay leaf, sugar, thyme and parsley. Simmer, uncovered, for 15 minutes or until reduced slightly. Remove bay leaf and parsley.

■ Add milk and cream; gently heat through but do not boil. Taste, add salt and adjust seasoning if desired. Serve in bowls. Makes about 8 servings.

*GARNISHES FOR SOUPS*

*For an attractive presentation, dress up soups with:*

- *Chopped fresh herbs: parsley, chives, tarragon, mint or basil*
- *Fresh flowers: chive or geranium*
- *Grated rind: lemon, orange or lime*
- *Seeds: roasted sunflower or sesame; celery seeds for pea soup*
- *Nuts, roasted and chopped*
- *Shredded cheeses, freshly grated Parmesan*
- *Creams: dollops of whipped cream or sour cream*
- *Spices: freshly grated nutmeg, coarsely ground pepper or red pepper flakes*

# Golden Vegetable Soup

*Serve this piping hot soup on a rainy fall day and bring the sunny warmth of summer vegetables to your table.*

| | | |
|---|---|---|
| 2 tbsp | vegetable oil | 25 mL |
| 1 | onion, minced | 1 |
| 2 cups | julienned peeled acorn or butternut squash | 500 mL |
| 1 cup | julienned carrots | 250 mL |
| 1/4 tsp | turmeric | 1 mL |
| 4 cups | chicken stock | 1 L |
| 1 | bay leaf | 1 |
| 1/4 tsp | dried thyme | 1 mL |
| 1 cup | corn | 250 mL |
| | Salt and pepper | |
| | Thyme sprigs | |

■ In large saucepan, heat oil over medium heat; cook onion until softened. Stir in squash, carrots and turmeric until vegetables are evenly colored yellow.

■ Add stock, bay leaf and thyme; reduce heat to low, cover and simmer for 10 minutes. Add corn; simmer for 5 minutes. Remove bay leaf; season with salt and pepper to taste. Ladle into soup bowls; garnish with thyme sprigs. Makes 6 to 8 servings.

# Bean, Zucchini and Pasta Soup

*This meal-in-a-bowl is ready in the time it takes to combine the ingredients. Round it out with whole-grain rolls and a few carrot sticks for crunch.*

| | | |
|---|---|---|
| 1 tbsp | butter or vegetable oil | 15 mL |
| 1/4 cup | finely chopped onion | 50 mL |
| 1 | clove garlic, minced | 1 |
| 1 | zucchini, chopped | 1 |
| 2 cups | chicken stock | 500 mL |
| 1 | can (14 oz/398 mL) tomatoes (undrained), chopped | 1 |
| 3/4 cup | broken spaghettini | 175 mL |
| 1/2 tsp | dried basil | 2 mL |
| 1 | can (14 oz/398 mL) kidney beans | 1 |
| | Salt and pepper | |

■ In large saucepan, melt butter over medium-high heat; sauté onion and garlic for 2 minutes or until tender. Stir in zucchini, chicken stock, tomatoes, spaghettini and basil. Bring to boil; cook for 8 minutes or until pasta is tender. Stir in kidney beans; cook for 1 minute or until heated through. Season with salt and pepper to taste. Makes 4 servings.

*Golden Vegetable Soup* ▶

# Cream of Watercress Soup

*Watercress makes a delicious and attractive cream soup.*

| | | |
|---|---|---|
| 2 tbsp | butter | 25 mL |
| 1/2 cup | finely chopped onion | 125 mL |
| 1/2 cup | grated peeled potato | 125 mL |
| 2 tbsp | minced fresh parsley | 25 mL |
| 2 cups | coarsely chopped watercress (about 1 bunch) | 500 mL |
| 2 cups | chicken stock | 500 mL |
| 1-1/2 tsp | fresh marjoram (or 1/2 tsp/2 mL dried) | 7 mL |
| 1 cup | light cream | 250 mL |
| | Salt and pepper | |

■ In saucepan, melt butter over medium-low heat; cook onion, potato and parsley, covered and stirring occasionally, until softened.

■ Add watercress, stock and marjoram; bring just to boil. Reduce heat to medium-low; cover and simmer for 30 minutes.

■ In blender or food processor, purée mixture until smooth; return to saucepan and bring to simmer. Reduce heat to medium-low and stir in cream just until heated through; do not boil. Season with salt and pepper to taste. Makes 4 servings.

# Fishermen's Chowder

*Supper's ready in 30 minutes with this nutritious chowder.*

| | | |
|---|---|---|
| 1 lb | boneless cod fillets (fresh or frozen) | 500 g |
| 1/4 lb | salt pork, diced | 125 g |
| 1/2 cup | finely chopped onion | 125 mL |
| 1/2 cup | chopped celery (optional) | 125 mL |
| 2 cups | diced peeled potatoes | 500 mL |
| 2 cups | water | 500 mL |
| 1 tsp | (approx) salt | 5 mL |
| Pinch | pepper | Pinch |
| 2 cups | milk | 500 mL |

■ Cut each cod fillet into 3 or 4 pieces. In large saucepan, cook pork over medium-high heat until crisp and browned. Reduce heat to medium and add onion and celery; cook until softened.

■ Add potatoes, water, salt and pepper; cover and cook for 10 minutes. Add fish and simmer gently until fish flakes easily when tested with fork, about 10 minutes. Add milk and heat through without boiling. Season with more salt and pepper to taste if desired. Makes about 6 servings.

# Goulash Soup

*A pound of stewing beef is the beginning of a delicious winter soup. Just add vegetables and seasonings and serve with crusty whole wheat rolls.*

| | | |
|---|---|---:|
| 2 tbsp | vegetable oil | 25 mL |
| 1 | onion, chopped | 1 |
| 1 lb | boneless stewing beef, cut in bite-size pieces | 500 g |
| 1 | clove garlic, minced | 1 |
| 1 tbsp | Hungarian sweet paprika | 15 mL |
| 1 tsp | caraway seeds | 5 mL |
| 1/2 tsp | salt | 2 mL |
| 4 cups | (approx) warm water | 1 L |
| 1 | tomato, peeled, seeded and chopped | 1 |
| 1 | sweet green pepper, seeded and sliced | 1 |
| 2 | potatoes, peeled and diced | 2 |
| | Chopped fresh parsley | |

■ In large saucepan, heat oil over medium-high heat; cook onion until tender. Add beef and cook, stirring, until browned all over.

■ Combine garlic, paprika, caraway seeds and salt; add to beef mixture and stir to combine. Return pan to heat and stir in water. Cover and simmer for 1 hour.

■ Stir in tomato and green pepper; cover and simmer for 30 minutes. Add potatoes and additional water if thinner soup is desired; simmer, covered, for 30 minutes. Taste and adjust seasoning if necessary. Garnish each serving with parsley. Makes 4 servings.

> *If you're using canned or dried stocks instead of homemade, wait until the end of the cooking time before seasoning with salt.*

# Italian Mussel Soup

*Mussels are a great wintertime food, and this soup is perfect for eating by the fireplace.*

| | | |
|---|---|---|
| 3 lb | mussels | 1.5 kg |
| 2 tbsp | each butter and vegetable oil | 25 mL |
| 1 | onion, chopped | 1 |
| 2 | cloves garlic, minced | 2 |
| 1 cup | dry white wine or chicken stock | 250 mL |
| 1 | can (28 oz/796 mL) tomatoes (undrained) | 1 |
| 1 tbsp | lemon juice | 15 mL |
| 1-1/2 tsp | dried basil | 7 mL |

■ Scrub mussels, removing any beards. Discard any mussels that don't close. Set aside.

■ In large heavy saucepan or Dutch oven, heat butter and oil over medium-high heat; cook onion and garlic until softened, about 4 minutes. Add wine, tomatoes, lemon juice and basil, crushing tomatoes with fork; bring to boil. Reduce heat and simmer for 5 minutes.

■ Add mussels; cover and cook for 5 to 7 minutes or until mussels have opened. Discard any that remain closed. Taste and adjust seasoning. Makes 8 servings.

# Cream of Leek and Green Pea Soup

*Serve this hearty soup in cups instead of bowls.*

| | | |
|---|---|---|
| 1 lb | leeks (white parts only), coarsely chopped | 500 g |
| 1 cup | green peas (fresh or frozen) | 250 mL |
| 1 cup | chicken stock | 250 mL |
| 1/4 cup | light cream | 50 mL |
| 1 tsp | lemon juice | 5 mL |
| | Salt and pepper | |
| | **GARNISH** | |
| 1/4 cup | plain yogurt | 50 mL |
| 1/4 cup | chopped fresh parsley | 50 mL |
| 1 | hard-cooked egg, chopped | 1 |

■ In large heavy saucepan, combine leeks, peas and stock; cover and cook over medium-low heat for about 15 minutes or until vegetables are tender.

■ In food processor or blender, purée soup until smooth; return to saucepan. Stir in cream and lemon juice; cook just until heated through. Season with salt and pepper to taste.

■ Pour soup into cups. Garnish each serving with dollop of yogurt; sprinkle with parsley and egg. Makes 4 servings.

*Italian Mussel Soup* ▶

# Buttermilk Soup in Pepper Shells

*Be sure to provide knives and forks along with soupspoons so your guests can eat their colorful red, green or yellow sweet pepper bowls after enjoying the creamy soup. Choose peppers that sit flat, or carefully shave the bottoms.*

| | | |
|---|---|---:|
| 8 | large sweet peppers | 8 |
| 4 cups | buttermilk | 1 L |
| 4 cups | plain yogurt | 1 L |
| 1 tsp | salt | 5 mL |
| | Pepper | |
| 2 tbsp | vegetable oil | 25 mL |
| 1 tbsp | black mustard seeds* or 2 tbsp (25 mL) sesame seeds | 15 mL |
| 1/4 cup | minced shallots | 50 mL |
| 2 tbsp | minced gingerroot | 25 mL |

■ Slice 1/2 inch (1 cm) from tops of sweet peppers; cut tops into julienne strips and set aside. Remove seeds and ribs from peppers, being careful not to pierce shells; set aside.

■ In large bowl, whisk together buttermilk, yogurt, salt, and pepper to taste; set aside.

■ In heavy skillet, heat oil over medium heat; cook mustard seeds just until they begin to pop (if using sesame seeds, just until lightly browned). Add shallots and gingerroot; cook for 2 to 3 minutes or until softened. Stir shallot mixture into buttermilk mixture; cover and refrigerate until chilled.

■ To serve, ladle soup into hollowed-out peppers; garnish with julienned pepper strips. Makes about 8 cups (2 L), enough to fill peppers twice.

*Available in Indian food stores and some supermarkets.

---

*STEP UP TO THE SOUP BAR*
*Soups are easy to make, simple to serve and economical. Because they gain flavor if made ahead, they're ideal for informal parties. Make several soups and have everyone choose right from the kettles in the kitchen or serve them from warmed tureens.*
*• Fresh vegetables and a creamy dip can be enjoyed while the soups heat. Serve an assortment of breads with the soups and follow with some cheese and fresh fruit for a satisfying meal.*

---

# Family Fish Chowder

*Creamed corn adds a touch of sweetness to this fish chowder, making it a favorite with children as well as adults.*

| | | |
|---|---|---|
| 5 | slices bacon, diced | 5 |
| 1 | large onion, diced | 1 |
| 1 | carrot, diced | 1 |
| 1 | stalk celery, diced | 1 |
| 1/2 cup | water | 125 mL |
| 1 lb | haddock, cut in bite-size chunks | 500 g |
| 2 cups | diced peeled potatoes | 500 mL |
| 4 cups | milk | 1 L |
| 1 | can (14 oz/398 mL) creamed corn | 1 |
| 1 tsp | salt | 5 mL |
| | Pepper | |

**GARNISH (optional)**

**Bacon bits, chopped green onions or chives**

■ In large saucepan, cook bacon until golden; drain off excess fat. Add onion, carrot and celery; cook until softened. Add water, fish and potatoes; cover and simmer for 10 minutes or until fish flakes easily when tested with fork and potatoes are tender. Add milk, corn, salt, and pepper to taste; heat through but do not boil. Garnish with bacon bits, onions or chives if desired. Makes 6 servings.

# Zucchini Soup with Herbs

*Serve this smooth and fragrant soup hot or enjoy any leftovers chilled the next day.*

| | | |
|---|---|---|
| 8 | zucchini (each 4 inches/10 cm long) | 8 |
| 2 tbsp | olive oil | 25 mL |
| 1 | leek, chopped | 1 |
| 4 cups | chicken stock | 1 L |
| 1/2 cup | dry white wine or chicken stock | 125 mL |
| 2 tbsp | finely chopped fresh tarragon (or 2 tsp/10 mL dried) | 25 mL |
| 2 tbsp | each finely chopped fresh parsley and chives | 25 mL |
| | Grated lemon rind | |

■ Peel and coarsely chop zucchini; set aside. In large saucepan, heat oil over medium heat; cook leek until softened. Add zucchini and reduce heat to low; cover and simmer for 10 minutes.

■ Transfer to blender or food processor fitted with steel blade; add 1 cup (250 mL) of the stock and purée until smooth. Return to saucepan; add wine and remaining stock. Mix together tarragon, parsley and chives; add half to soup, reserving remaining herbs for garnish. Cover; simmer over low heat for 5 minutes. Ladle into bowls; sprinkle with lemon rind and remaining herbs. Makes about 8 servings.

# French Onion Soup

*This savory soup is delicious for lunch or as the first course to a special dinner.*
*This is very cheesy, so use less cheese than called for if you wish.*

| | | |
|---|---|---|
| 1/4 cup | butter | 50 mL |
| 4 | onions, thinly sliced | 4 |
| 1/4 cup | all-purpose flour | 50 mL |
| 4 cups | beef stock | 1 L |
| 1/4 cup | dry white wine | 50 mL |
| | Salt and pepper | |
| 4 | slices French bread, toasted | 4 |
| 2 cups | (approx) shredded Gruyère cheese (8 oz/250 g) | 500 mL |

■ In large heavy saucepan, melt butter over medium-low heat; cook onions until tender, about 10 minutes. Sprinkle with flour; cook, stirring, for 5 minutes. Gradually add beef stock and wine, stirring constantly; simmer gently for 15 minutes. Season with salt and pepper to taste.

■ Pour soup into 4 ovenproof soup bowls. Place 1 slice French bread in each; sprinkle with cheese. Broil 3 inches (7 cm) from heat until cheese is golden brown and bubbling. Makes 4 servings.

---

*CROUTONS*
*Croutons add an interesting contrast of flavor, color and texture to all soups and chowders.*
*• Spread 3 cups (750 mL) bread cubes on rimmed baking sheet. Bake in 300°F (150°C) oven for 10 to 15 minutes.*
*• In large skillet, melt 1/3 cup (75 mL) butter. Stir in bread cubes, tossing to coat well. Return cubes to baking sheet; bake for 15 minutes or until crisp and lightly browned. Let cool. Makes 3 cups (750 mL).*
*• Garlic Croutons: Add 1 clove garlic, minced, to melted butter.*
*• Parmesan Croutons: Add 2 tbsp (25 mL) grated Parmesan cheese to melted butter.*
*• Herb Croutons: Add 1 tsp (5 mL) dried parsley, chives, Italian seasoning or favorite herb to melted butter.*

# Spinach Soup

*Liven up spinach soup with basil, garlic, walnuts and cheese.*

| | | |
|---|---|---|
| 6 cups | chicken stock | 1.5 L |
| 1 cup | fine egg noodles or shell pasta (about 2 oz/60 g) | 250 mL |
| 2 cups | chopped fresh spinach | 500 mL |
| 1/2 cup | chopped fresh parsley | 125 mL |
| 1/2 cup | fresh basil leaves | 125 mL |
| 1/4 cup | walnuts or almonds | 50 mL |
| 1/4 cup | (approx) freshly grated Parmesan cheese | 50 mL |
| 1 | clove garlic, minced | 1 |
| 1/4 cup | olive oil | 50 mL |
| | Salt and pepper | |

■ In large saucepan, bring 5 cups (1.25 L) of the stock to boil. Add noodles and simmer, covered, until tender but firm. Remove from heat.

■ Meanwhile, in blender or food processor, process spinach, parsley and remaining stock until smooth. Add basil, walnuts, Parmesan and garlic; process for 1 minute. Blend in oil until smooth.

■ Stir spinach mixture into saucepan and heat through. Season with salt and pepper to taste. Ladle into bowls and sprinkle with more Parmesan if desired. Makes 6 servings.

# Strawberry Soup

*This soup makes a refreshing summer drink, a light starter for brunch or a sweet ending to a meal when garnished with whipped cream.*

| | | |
|---|---|---|
| 4 cups | strawberries, hulled | 1 L |
| 1 cup | peach nectar | 250 mL |
| 1 tbsp | kirsch or apricot brandy | 15 mL |
| | **GARNISH** | |
| | Whipped cream, sliced strawberry and mint leaves | |

■ In blender or food processor, purée strawberries until smooth. Strain through fine sieve into bowl, discarding seeds. Stir in peach nectar and kirsch.

■ **Garnish:** Serve soup in chilled bowls or glasses; garnish with dollop of whipped cream, slice of strawberry and mint leaves. Makes 4 servings.

# Split Pea Soup with Sausage Balls

*After cross-country skiing, everyone will enjoy steaming soup, served with crusty rolls and pâté.*

| | | |
|---|---|---:|
| 8 cups | chicken stock | 2 L |
| 2 cups | green split peas | 500 mL |
| 1 cup | diced carrots | 250 mL |
| 1 cup | diced peeled potato | 250 mL |
| 1 cup | diced celery and leaves | 250 mL |
| 1 cup | chopped onion | 250 mL |
| 1/2 tsp | dried thyme | 2 mL |
| 1/4 tsp | dried savory | 1 mL |
| | Salt and pepper | |
| | **SAUSAGE BALLS** | |
| 1 lb | bulk sausage | 500 g |
| 1/4 cup | chopped fresh parsley | 50 mL |
| 1/2 tsp | salt | 2 mL |
| 1/2 tsp | dried thyme | 2 mL |
| 4 tsp | vegetable oil | 20 mL |

■ **Sausage Balls:** In bowl, mix sausage, parsley, salt and thyme; shape into 3/4-inch (2 cm) balls. In large nonstick skillet, heat oil over medium heat; cook sausage balls, in batches if necessary, until browned all over, about 5 minutes. Set aside.

■ In large heavy saucepan or Dutch oven, bring stock to boil; gradually add split peas. Skim off foam. Add sausage balls; reduce heat, cover and simmer for 30 minutes or until peas are tender. Add carrots, potato, celery, onion, thyme and savory; simmer, covered, until vegetables are tender, about 15 minutes. Season with salt and pepper to taste. Makes 6 to 8 servings.

# Cucumber Yogurt Soup

*Cucumbers, yogurt and dill are as cooling in summer soups as they are in salads.*

| | | |
|---|---|---:|
| 2 | cucumbers, peeled, seeded and chopped | 2 |
| 1/2 cup | chopped onions | 125 mL |
| 1-1/2 cups | plain yogurt | 375 mL |
| 1/2 cup | chicken stock | 125 mL |
| | Salt and pepper | |
| | Chopped fresh dill | |

■ In food processor or blender, process cucumbers and onions until smooth; blend in yogurt and stock. Season with salt and pepper to taste. Transfer to bowl; cover and refrigerate until chilled. Sprinkle with dill. Makes 4 servings.

# Fiesta Dip

*Serve this spicy dip warm with crudités and tortilla or corn chips. You can use 1 lb (500 g) softened cream cheese instead of the Velveeta cheese if you like.*

| | | |
|---|---|---|
| 1 lb | Velveeta cheese, shredded | 500 g |
| 1/2 lb | old Cheddar cheese, shredded | 250 g |
| 4 | large tomatoes, seeded and finely chopped | 4 |
| 1 | can (4 oz/110 g) jalapeño peppers, drained, seeded and chopped | 1 |
| 1 | onion, finely chopped | 1 |
| 4 | cloves garlic, minced | 4 |

■ In 6-cup (1.5 L) casserole, combine Velveeta and Cheddar cheeses, tomatoes, peppers, onion and garlic; bake in 350°F (180°C) oven for 1 hour or until bubbling. Let cool slightly and serve. *(Dip can be covered and refrigerated for up to 2 days or frozen for up to 1 month. To serve, reheat in 350°F/180°C oven for 30 to 35 minutes, longer if frozen, or until bubbling.)* Makes about 4 cups (1 L).

# Make-Ahead Hot or Cold Seafood Bites

*Offer this hot on crackers or cold in hollowed-out cherry tomatoes.*

| | | |
|---|---|---|
| 1 lb | cream cheese | 500 g |
| 1 tbsp | lemon juice | 15 mL |
| 2 tsp | light cream | 10 mL |
| 1 tsp | minced onion | 5 mL |
| 1/2 tsp | minced garlic | 2 mL |
| 1/4 tsp | Worcestershire sauce | 1 mL |
| 1 | can (6.5 oz/184 g) tuna, drained and flaked | 1 |
| 1 | can (4 oz/113 g) shrimp, drained and chopped | 1 |
| 1 | can (104 g) smoked oysters, drained and chopped | 1 |
| | Melba rounds, crisp wafers or cherry tomatoes | |

■ In bowl, combine cheese, lemon juice, cream, onion, garlic and Worcestershire sauce; divide among 3 small bowls.

■ To first bowl, add tuna; mix well. To second bowl, stir in shrimp; mix well. To third bowl, stir in oysters; mix well. Using piping bag or teaspoon, pipe or mound mixture in 1-inch (2.5 cm) rounds onto baking sheets. Freeze until firm; store in airtight containers in freezer.

■ To serve hot, place frozen mounds on melba rounds; bake in 375°F (190°C) oven for 10 minutes or until bubbly. To serve cold, thaw and spoon into hollowed-out cherry tomatoes. Makes about 60 appetizers.

*Fiesta Dip* ▶

# Chicken Liver Pâté

*While company is just arriving, serve this intriguing pâté on melba toast and watch it disappear. This pâté also freezes well, so pack away some of it for future occasions.*

| | | |
|---|---|---|
| 1/2 cup | butter | 125 mL |
| 1/2 cup | chopped onions | 125 mL |
| 1/2 cup | chopped peeled apple | 125 mL |
| 1 lb | chicken livers, trimmed and halved | 500 g |
| 1 | bay leaf | 1 |
| 1 tsp | salt | 5 mL |
| 1/2 tsp | pepper | 2 mL |
| 1/2 tsp | each dried thyme and marjoram (or 1 tsp/5 mL each chopped fresh) | 2 mL |
| 2 tbsp | whipping cream | 25 mL |
| 1/4 cup | butter, softened | 50 mL |
| 2 tsp | brandy | 10 mL |
| | Salt and pepper | |

■ In skillet, melt 1/4 cup (50 mL) of the butter over medium heat; cook onions for 3 minutes. Add apple; cook until apple and onions are translucent. Transfer to blender.

■ Add remaining 1/4 cup (50 mL) butter to skillet; heat until foaming but not browned. Add livers, bay leaf, salt, pepper, thyme and marjoram; cook, stirring, for 6 to 8 minutes or until livers are browned but still slightly pink inside. Remove bay leaf. Add liver mixture to blender; process until smooth. Add cream; process to blend. (For very smooth paste, press mixture through fine sieve.) Let cool. Gradually blend in butter; blend in brandy, and salt and pepper to taste.

■ Pack into containers; press waxed paper or plastic wrap onto surface of pâté. Refrigerate for at least 4 hours or up to 3 days. Makes about 3 cups (750 mL).

# Multilayered Mexican Dip

*Serve this popular party dip with tortilla chips. For our photograph, we sprinkled cheese around the edge of the dish, made a ring of green onions, then black olives and placed chopped tomatoes in the centre.*

| | | |
|---|---|---:|
| 1 | can (14 oz/398 mL) refried beans | 1 |
| 1-1/4 cups | sour cream | 300 mL |
| 1/4 tsp | salt | 1 mL |
| 1/4 tsp | cumin | 1 mL |
| Dash | hot pepper sauce | Dash |
| 2 | ripe avocados | 2 |
| 1/3 cup | finely chopped onion | 75 mL |
| 1 tbsp | lime juice | 15 mL |
| 1/4 tsp | hot pepper flakes | 1 mL |
| 1/3 cup | sliced green onions | 75 mL |
| 1/2 cup | sliced pitted black olives | 125 mL |
| 2 | tomatoes, chopped | 2 |
| 2 cups | shredded Cheddar cheese | 500 mL |

■ In bowl, blend together beans, 1/4 cup (50 mL) of the sour cream, salt, cumin and hot pepper sauce; spread evenly over tray 12 inches (30 cm) in diameter and at least 1-1/2 inches (4 cm) deep.

■ Peel and pit avocados. In bowl, mash together avocados, chopped onion, 1/4 cup (50 mL) of the sour cream, lime juice and pepper flakes; spread over refried bean layer. Spread remaining sour cream over top, completely covering avocado layer. Garnish with concentric rings of green onions on outside, then black olives, tomatoes and cheese. Cover and refrigerate until serving for up to 8 hours. Makes about 24 servings.

# *Easy Salmon Mousse*

*For our photograph, we prepared this in a ring mould. You can, however, use any 6-cup (1.5 L) mould; it's particularly attractive in a fish-shaped one. Serve with pumpernickel or French bread.*

| | | |
|---|---|---|
| 2 | **envelopes unflavored gelatin** | 2 |
| 1/2 cup | **water** | 125 mL |
| 3 | **cans (each 7-3/4 oz/220 g) salmon, drained** | 3 |
| 1-1/2 cups | **sour cream** | 375 mL |
| 1/4 cup | **chopped fresh dill** | 50 mL |
| 1/4 cup | **lemon juice** | 50 mL |
| 2 tbsp | **minced onion** | 25 mL |
| 2 tbsp | **chopped drained capers** | 25 mL |
| 1 tsp | **salt** | 5 mL |
| 1/2 tsp | **hot pepper sauce** | 2 mL |
| 1/4 tsp | **paprika** | 1 mL |
| 1 cup | **whipping cream, whipped** | 250 mL |

■ In small saucepan, sprinkle gelatin over water; let stand for 5 minutes to soften. Heat gently until gelatin is dissolved.

■ In blender or food processor, combine salmon, sour cream, dill, lemon juice, onion, capers, salt, hot pepper sauce and paprika. Pour in gelatin mixture and purée until smooth. Transfer to bowl; fold in whipped cream.

■ Turn mixture into 6-cup (1.5 L) mould. Chill until firm, at least 1 hour. *(Mousse can be refrigerated for up to 1 week.)* Unmould by quickly dipping bottom of mould into hot water; turn out onto serving platter. Makes 8 to 10 servings.

# Miniature Artichoke Tarts

*These savory mini-quiches are always a hit with guests. Serve them hot from the oven or let cool and reheat just before serving.*

| | | |
|---|---|---|
| 2 | jars (each 6 oz/170 mL) marinated artichoke hearts | 2 |
| 1 | onion, finely chopped | 1 |
| 1 | large clove garlic, minced | 1 |
| 4 | eggs | 4 |
| 1/4 cup | fine dry bread crumbs | 50 mL |
| 1/2 tsp | salt | 2 mL |
| 1/4 tsp | dried oregano | 1 mL |
| Dash | hot pepper sauce | Dash |
| | Pepper | |
| 2 cups | shredded old Cheddar cheese | 500 mL |

■ Drain artichokes, reserving 1/4 cup (50 mL) marinade. Chop artichokes into 1/2-inch (1 cm) pieces; set aside.

■ In skillet, heat reserved marinade; cook onion and garlic until softened, about 5 minutes.

■ In bowl, beat eggs; stir in onion mixture, bread crumbs, salt, oregano, hot pepper sauce, and pepper to taste. Blend in cheese; stir in artichokes.

■ Spoon mixture into well-greased or nonstick 1-3/4-inch (4 cm) tart tins, filling about two-thirds full. Bake in 325°F (160°C) oven for 10 to 15 minutes or until set. Makes about 36.

# Fruit-and-Nut Cheese Spread

*If apricots are very dry, cover with boiling water for about 15 minutes to plump them up. Spoon this spread into a serving bowl instead of a flan pan if desired. Serve it with apple slices, pear wedges or crackers.*

| | | |
|---|---|---|
| 3 cups | shredded Cheddar cheese | 750 mL |
| 1/2 lb | cream cheese | 250 g |
| 1/4 cup | sherry or milk | 50 mL |
| 1/2 cup | coarsely chopped walnuts | 125 mL |
| 1/2 cup | golden raisins | 125 mL |
| 1/2 cup | chopped dried apricots | 125 mL |
| 1/4 cup | chopped dates | 50 mL |

■ In food processor or by hand, blend together Cheddar, cream cheese and sherry until smooth. Using on/off motion, add walnuts, raisins, apricots and dates.

■ Line bottom of 8-inch (20 cm) flan pan with removable bottom with foil. Pack cheese mixture into pan. Cover with plastic wrap; refrigerate for several hours or overnight.

■ At serving time, remove plastic wrap; invert pan onto serving plate. Remove pan; lift off foil. Makes 10 to 12 servings.

# Ricotta, Ham and Spinach Phyllo Triangles

*Only the spinach in this simple phyllo filling needs precooking. The finished product makes a wonderful finger food starter for any occasion.*

| | | |
|---|---|---|
| 1 | **pkg (1 lb/454 g) phyllo pastry, thawed** | 1 |
| **1 cup** | **butter, melted** | **250 mL** |
| | **FILLING** | |
| **2 cups** | **packed fresh spinach, cooked, squeezed dry and chopped** | **500 mL** |
| **2 cups** | **ricotta cheese** | **500 mL** |
| **1-1/2 cups** | **shredded cooked ham (such as Black Forest), about 8 oz/250 g** | **375 mL** |
| **1/2 cup** | **freshly grated Parmesan cheese or shredded old Cheddar cheese** | **125 mL** |
| **2 tsp** | **chopped fresh tarragon (or 1/2 tsp/2 mL dried)** | **10 mL** |
| **4** | **egg yolks** | **4** |
| | **Salt and pepper** | |

■ **Filling:** In large bowl, blend together spinach, ricotta, ham, cheese, tarragon, egg yolks, and salt and pepper to taste.

■ Place 1 sheet of phyllo on work surface, covering remaining phyllo with waxed paper then damp tea towel to prevent drying. Brush sheet lightly with butter; lay second sheet over top and brush with butter. Using ruler and sharp knife, cut pastry crosswise into 3-1/2-inch (9 cm) wide strips.

■ Spoon rounded tablespoonful (15 mL) filling about 1 inch (2.5 cm) from end of each strip. Fold 1 corner of phyllo over filling so bottom edge of phyllo meets side edge to form triangle. Fold up triangle. Continue folding triangle sideways and upward until end of phyllo strip is reached. Press edges firmly together. Repeat with remaining phyllo sheets and filling.

■ Place triangles on lightly greased baking sheets; brush with butter. Bake in 375°F (190°C) oven for 15 to 20 minutes or until puffed and golden. Makes about 50 hors d'oeuvres.

---

*PHYLLO PASTRY TRIANGLES*
*You can prepare triangles ahead of time, but don't brush uncooked packages with melted butter. Freeze in a single layer on an ungreased baking sheet. Pack carefully into airtight containers with rigid sides. Do not thaw before baking. Place on lightly greased baking sheet; brush with butter and bake in 375°F (190°C) oven until puffed and golden, 25 to 35 minutes. Baked phyllo triangles can also be reheated in 350°F (180°C) oven for 5 to 10 minutes.*

# Microwave Picnic Pâté

*Foods such as meat loaf or pâté can be microwaved more evenly when prepared in a ring mould. Because this dish can't be stirred, be sure to rotate it during the cooking time. Test with a meat thermometer in several places to make sure it is evenly cooked through.*

| | | |
|---|---|---|
| 1 | onion, finely chopped | 1 |
| 1 | clove garlic, minced | 1 |
| 1 tbsp | butter | 15 mL |
| 1/2 lb | ground pork | 250 g |
| 1/2 lb | ground veal | 250 g |
| 1/4 lb | baby beef liver, finely diced | 125 g |
| 1/2 cup | coarsely chopped cooked ham (3 oz/90 g) | 125 mL |
| 1 | egg, lightly beaten | 1 |
| 1 tsp | coarsely ground pepper | 5 mL |
| 3/4 tsp | salt | 4 mL |
| 1/2 tsp | allspice | 2 mL |
| 1/4 tsp | dried thyme | 1 mL |
| 6 | slices bacon (1/3 lb/175 g) | 6 |
| 3 | bay leaves | 3 |

■ In large bowl, microwave onion, garlic and butter at High for 3 minutes or until softened, stirring once. Add pork, veal, liver, ham, egg, pepper, salt, allspice and thyme; mix well.

■ Line bottom and sides of 4- or 6-cup (1 or 1.5 L) ring mould with bacon, letting ends hang over side of pan. (Alternatively, use 9-inch/23 cm pie plate with inverted custard cup in centre.) Tuck bay leaves under bacon. Pack meat mixture evenly into mould; fold ends of bacon over meat mixture.

■ Cover with vented plastic wrap and microwave at High for 5 minutes, rotating once. Microwave at Medium-High (70%) for 4 minutes or until thermometer or meat probe inserted in several places registers 170°F (75°C) and juices are no longer pink, rotating once. Let stand for 5 minutes. Pour off and reserve juices; let pâté and juices cool. Remove congealed fat on juices; refrigerate juices.

■ Cover and refrigerate pâté for 12 hours. To serve, invert onto serving plate; remove bay leaves. Brush pâté with reserved juices; cut into 1/2-inch (1 cm) thick slices. *(Pâté can be refrigerated for up to 4 days.)* Makes 8 appetizer servings.

# Brie and Red Pepper Mini-Quiches

*The combination of cheese, red pepper and crumbled bacon makes a delicious taste sensation.*

| | Pastry for double-crust pie | |
|---|---|---|
| 2 tbsp | butter | 25 mL |
| 3/4 cup | finely chopped sweet red peppers | 175 mL |
| 1/2 lb | Brie cheese, cut in small cubes | 250 g |
| 10 | slices bacon, cooked and crumbled | 10 |
| 3 | eggs | 3 |
| 1-1/3 cups | whipping cream | 325 mL |
| | Salt and cayenne pepper | |

■ On lightly floured surface, roll out pastry thinly and line thirty-six 2-1/4-inch (6 cm) tartlet tins. Line with foil and weight down with pie weights or dried beans. Bake in 375°F (190°C) oven for 10 minutes. Remove foil and pie weights; let cool.

■ In skillet, melt butter; sauté red peppers until softened. Spoon into tart shells; top with cheese, then bacon.

■ In bowl, beat together eggs and cream; season with salt and cayenne to taste. Pour over mixture in tart shells; bake in 350°F (180°C) oven for 10 to 15 minutes or until filling is firm. Serve immediately. *(Tarts can be cooled and frozen in airtight containers. To reheat, bake frozen tartlets in 375°F/190°C oven for 10 minutes or until heated through.)* Makes 36 appetizers.

---

*PÂTÉS*

*Pâtés were originally sealed in a dough-like paste (called* pâte *in French) to contain moisture and flavor. Today, pâtés range all the way from the traditional meat mixtures (coarse or smooth) to a wide variety of baked or unbaked moulds of fish, seafood, poultry and even vegetables.*

# Two-Way Devilled Eggs

*Devilled eggs are one of summer's best treats.*

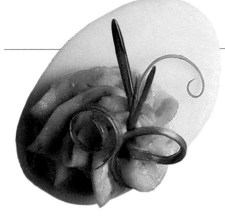

■ Place eggs in single layer in saucepan; pour in enough cold water to come 1 inch (2.5 cm) above eggs. Bring to boil; remove from heat. Cover and let stand for 25 minutes. Drain eggs; immerse in cold water until cool. Peel and halve eggs.

■ Transfer half of the egg yolks to bowl; transfer remaining egg yolks to separate bowl.

■ **Salmon Filling:** To one bowl of yolks, add salmon, mayonnaise, salt and hot pepper sauce; mash together until very smooth, adding more mayonnaise if necessary. Spoon into piping bag fitted with fluted tip; pipe into 12 egg halves. Garnish with green onion.

■ **Peppery Mustard Filling:** To other bowl of yolks, add jalapeño pepper, mayonnaise, mustard and salt; mash together until very smooth, adding more mayonnaise if necessary. Spoon into piping bag fitted with fluted tip; pipe into remaining eggs. Garnish with thyme. Makes 24 appetizers.

| | | |
|---|---|---|
| 12 | eggs | 12 |

**SALMON FILLING**

| | | |
|---|---|---|
| 1 | can (3-3/4 oz/106 g) sockeye salmon, drained | 1 |
| 3 tbsp | (approx) mayonnaise | 50 mL |
| 1/2 tsp | salt | 2 mL |
| Dash | hot pepper sauce | Dash |
| | Chopped green onion or fresh parsley | |

**PEPPERY MUSTARD FILLING**

| | | |
|---|---|---|
| 1 | pickled jalapeño pepper, minced | 1 |
| 4 tsp | (approx) mayonnaise | 20 mL |
| 1 tsp | Dijon mustard | 5 mL |
| 1/2 tsp | salt | 2 mL |
| | Thyme sprigs | |

# Stuffed Jumbo Shrimp

*These appetizers look beautiful when the filling is piped on.*

| | | |
|---|---|---|
| 24 | large raw shrimp (1-1/2 lb/750 g) | 24 |
| 8 cups | water | 2 L |
| 1 | carrot, sliced | 1 |
| 1 | stalk celery, sliced | 1 |
| 1 | onion, sliced | 1 |
| 1 | sprig fresh parsley | 1 |
| | Salt and pepper | |
| | **FILLING** | |
| 3/4 lb | cream cheese | 375 g |
| 2 tbsp | each chopped fresh parsley and dill | 25 mL |
| 1 tbsp | lemon juice | 15 mL |
| 1 tbsp | sour cream | 15 mL |
| 1 | green onion, chopped | 1 |
| 1 tsp | dried tarragon | 5 mL |
| | **GARNISH** | |
| 1/2 cup | chopped fresh parsley | 125 mL |

■ Peel and devein shrimp, leaving tails on for attractive garnish.

■ In large saucepan, combine water, carrot, celery, onion, parsley, and salt and pepper to taste; bring to boil. Reduce heat and simmer for 10 minutes. Strain and return liquid to pan; bring to boil and add shrimp. Cook for 2 to 3 minutes or just until shrimp begin to curl and turn pink; remove from liquid and let cool. (Freeze liquid for another use, such as in fish sauces or soups.)

■ **Filling:** In food processor or mixing bowl, combine cream cheese, parsley, dill, lemon juice, sour cream, onion and tarragon; process until combined.

■ To assemble, cut slit along outer curve of shrimp, deep enough to hold filling. Using piping bag, pipe filling down slit in shrimp. To garnish, dip the filled side into parsley; arrange on serving platter. Makes 24 appetizers.

---

*CUCUMBER-SHRIMP CANAPÉS*
*Here's a tasty cocktail snack that takes only minutes to make. Run tines of fork lengthwise along unpeeled seedless cucumber to make decorative edge. Cut cucumber into 1/4-inch (5 mm) thick slices. On each slice, spoon a dab of mayonnaise. Top with a small cooked shrimp (shelled and deveined) and a little fresh dill, mint or chive.*

# Hot Cheese Wafers

*Keep a supply of these in your freezer, ready to pop into the oven for unexpected company.*

| | | |
|---|---|---|
| 2 cups | shredded old orange Cheddar cheese | 500 mL |
| 1/2 cup | all-purpose flour | 125 mL |
| 1/4 cup | butter, softened | 50 mL |

■ In food processor or mixing bowl, process cheese, flour and butter until well mixed. Wrap and refrigerate for about 30 minutes. Shape into small balls, about 1 tsp (5 mL) each. *(Cheese balls can be frozen; thaw before baking.)*

■ Arrange about 2 inches (5 cm) apart on baking sheets; flatten with tines of fork. Bake in 400°F (200°C) oven for 6 to 8 minutes or until firm but not browned, being careful not to overbake. Serve hot or let cool on rack. Makes 3 to 4 dozen.

# Smoked Trout Mousse

*Serve this mousse with dark pumpernickel bread or whole wheat melba toast. If desired, you can substitute two cans (104 g each) of smoked oysters, well drained, for the trout.*

| | | |
|---|---|---|
| 1/2 lb | smoked trout fillets | 250 g |
| 2 tbsp | chopped fresh dill | 25 mL |
| 2 tbsp | unsalted butter | 25 mL |
| 2 tsp | lemon juice | 10 mL |
| Dash | hot pepper sauce | Dash |

| | | |
|---|---|---|
| 1/2 cup | whipping cream | 125 mL |
| 1 tbsp | tomato paste | 15 mL |

■ In food processor or blender, combine trout, dill, butter, lemon juice and hot pepper sauce; process until smooth. With machine running, gradually add cream through feed tube, processing until smooth and creamy. Add tomato paste; process just until blended.

■ Spoon mousse into serving dish. Cover and refrigerate for at least 1 hour or until chilled. Makes about 1-1/2 cups (375 mL).

# Pepper-Crusted Tenderloin Slices

*Slices of grilled tenderloin served warm or at room temperature with a dipping sauce make an unusual teaser to serve with mixed drinks.*

■ Wipe tenderloins with damp cloth; place on waxed paper. Spread half of the chutney over one side of tenderloins; sprinkle with half of the pepper. Turn tenderloins over and repeat with remaining chutney and pepper.

■ Bake in greased baking dish in 375°F (190°C) oven for 20 minutes; turn over and bake for 20 to 30 minutes longer or until meat thermometer registers 170°F (75°C). (Alternatively, place on lightly greased grill 5 inches/ 12 cm from hot coals, or at high setting. Grill, turning once, for 20 to 25 minutes.) To serve, slice into 3/4-inch (2 cm) thick rounds.

■ **Sauce:** In small serving bowl, combine sour cream and chutney; pass as dipping sauce. Makes about 24 appetizers.

| | | |
|---|---|---|
| 3 | pork tenderloins (about 3/4 lb/375 g each) | 3 |
| 1/2 cup | mango chutney | 125 mL |
| 3 tbsp | coarse black pepper | 50 mL |
| | **SAUCE** | |
| 1/2 cup | sour cream | 125 mL |
| 1/3 cup | mango chutney | 75 mL |

# Shrimp Pie

*This fancy spread combines the flavors of shrimp cocktail and cream cheese.*

| | | |
|---|---|---|
| 1/2 lb | cream cheese | 250 g |
| 1/3 cup | sour cream | 75 mL |
| 1/3 cup | ketchup | 75 mL |
| 1 tsp | horseradish | 5 mL |
| 1/2 lb | small cooked shrimp, shelled and deveined | 250 g |
| | Crackers | |

■ In food processor or mixing bowl, process cream cheese and sour cream until smooth. Spread in 9-inch (23 cm) glass pie plate; chill until firm.

■ Mix together ketchup and horseradish; spread over cheese layer. Arrange shrimp on top. Serve with crackers. Makes about 3 cups (750 mL).

# Parmesan Chicken Nibbles

*Chicken wings can be separated into three sections. The wing tips can be used to make chicken stock. The second sections make great finger food and the last sections look like small drumsticks when the bone is scraped to mount the meat at one end. If desired, you can use small drumsticks for heartier fare.*

| | | | | | |
|---|---|---|---|---|---|
| 2 lb | chicken wings | 1 kg | 1 tsp | paprika | 5 mL |
| 1 cup | freshly grated Parmesan cheese | 250 mL | 1 cup | plain yogurt | 250 mL |
| 2 tbsp | chopped fresh rosemary (or 2 tsp/10 mL crumbled dried) | 25 mL | | | |

■ Separate wings at joints. In bowl, combine Parmesan, rosemary and paprika. Place yogurt in separate bowl. Dip chicken into yogurt, then into cheese mixture to coat.

■ Arrange wings in single layer on greased rack set on baking sheet. Bake in 375°F (190°C) oven for about 20 minutes or until tender and no longer pink inside. Makes about 2 dozen.

---

*CRUDITÉS*

*Crunchy crudités, or raw vegetables, are satisfying on their own or served with flavorful dips such as Creamy Dill Dip (p. 56) or Fiesta Dip (p. 40).*

*• Arrange vegetables of various flavors and colors in brandy glasses or flowered crockery, or just toss them together in a big salad bowl or glass jug.*

*• The vegetables are usually served raw but may be blanched briefly in boiling water until tender-crisp, then chilled in ice water.*

*• Dips for crudités can be either hot or cold. Hot dips can be served in a fondue pot. Or use hollowed out vegetables as interesting dip containers. Big green peppers and tomatoes or zucchini and cucumbers halved lengthwise are ideal.*

*• Bread sticks and crackers add interest and flavor variety to any crudités arrangement.*

# Curried Popcorn

*Enjoy this low-cal snack with your favorite home movies.*

| | | |
|---|---|---|
| 8 cups | popped popcorn (about 1/2 cup/125 mL unpopped) | 2 L |
| 2 tbsp | butter | 25 mL |
| 1 tsp | curry powder | 5 mL |
| Pinch | cayenne pepper | Pinch |

■ Place popcorn in serving bowl. In small saucepan or microwaveable measuring cup, melt butter; stir in curry powder and cayenne. Drizzle over popcorn, tossing gently. Makes 8 cups (2 L).

# Red Pepper Bruschetta

*Crusty bread topped with a light tomato and garlic mixture, traditional bruschetta makes a satisfying appetizer. This version, with a colorful red pepper topping, is loaded with flavor.*

| | | |
|---|---|---|
| 1/4 cup | olive oil | 50 mL |
| 2 | cloves garlic, minced | 2 |
| 1 | small red onion, diced | 1 |
| 3 | sweet red peppers, peeled and diced | 3 |
| 2 tbsp | chopped fresh basil or parsley | 25 mL |
| | Salt and pepper | |
| 1 | stick French bread (baguette) | 1 |
| 1/3 cup | freshly grated Parmesan cheese | 75 mL |

■ In skillet, heat half of the oil over medium heat; cook garlic and onion for 4 to 5 minutes or until tender but not browned. Add red peppers; cook for 5 to 8 minutes or until fragrant and wilted. Stir in basil. Season with salt and pepper to taste. *(Recipe can be prepared to this point, covered and refrigerated for up to 2 days.)*

■ Cut bread diagonally into 1-inch (2.5 cm) thick slices to make about 12 slices. Arrange in single layer on baking sheet. Brush with remaining oil; broil for 1 to 2 minutes or until crisp and browned. Turn slices over and spoon red pepper mixture over bread; sprinkle with Parmesan.

■ Bake in 400°F (200°C) oven for 10 minutes or until heated through. Makes 6 servings.

# Creamy Dill Dip

*Kids will love fresh crisp vegetables when the crunchy sticks and florets are dunked in this dip.*

| | | | | |
|---|---|---|---|---|
| 1 cup | creamed cottage cheese | 250 mL | | Carrot and celery sticks |
| 1/2 cup | sour cream or plain yogurt | 125 mL | | Cauliflower and broccoli florets |
| 2 tbsp | finely chopped green onions or chives | 25 mL | | Cherry tomatoes |
| 2 tbsp | chopped fresh dill (or 2 tsp/10 mL dried dillweed) | 25 mL | | |
| 1 tsp | lemon juice | 5 mL | | |
| | Salt and pepper | | | |

■ In food processor or blender, combine cottage cheese with sour cream; process until smooth. Transfer to bowl; stir in onion, dill, lemon juice, and salt and pepper to taste. Cover and refrigerate for 2 hours or until chilled. Serve with vegetables. Makes about 1-1/2 cups (375 mL).

# Hummus

*Serve this Middle Eastern dip with fresh vegetables and warm pita bread or pita crisps. Easy to make, this dip is a good source of fibre and protein. Tahini (sesame seed paste) is available at many health food stores.*

| | | | | | |
|---|---|---|---|---|---|
| 3 | cloves garlic | 3 | 1/4 cup | tahini or peanut butter | 50 mL |
| 1 | can (19 oz/540 mL) chick-peas, drained | 1 | 3 tbsp | lemon juice | 50 mL |
| | | | 2 tbsp | vegetable oil | 25 mL |
| | | | 2 tbsp | water | 25 mL |
| | | | 1 tsp | cumin | 5 mL |
| | | | 1/2 tsp | salt | 2 mL |

*PITA CRISPS*

*Split 2 pita breads (about 6 inches/15 cm in diameter) to make 4 rounds. In small bowl, microwave 1/4 cup (50 mL) butter at High for 40 to 60 seconds or until melted; brush lightly over each round. Cut each round into 8 triangles; arrange half in single layer on paper towel. Microwave at High for 2-1/2 to 3 minutes or until crisp. Repeat with remaining triangles. Makes 32 crisps.*

■ In food processor, mince garlic. Add chick-peas, tahini, lemon juice, oil, water, cumin and salt; process until smooth. Taste and adjust seasoning if necessary. Transfer to serving bowl. Makes about 1-1/2 cups (375 mL).

# Beef and Onion Rolls

*These sweet-and-sour rolls make great after-theatre snacks.*

| | | |
|---|---|---|
| 1/2 lb | top round or sirloin steak (about 2 inches/ 5 cm thick) | 250 g |
| 2 tbsp | light soy sauce | 25 mL |
| 2 tbsp | vegetable oil | 25 mL |
| 1 tbsp | packed brown sugar | 15 mL |
| 1 tbsp | rice vinegar | 15 mL |
| 1 tbsp | water | 15 mL |
| 10 | green onions | 10 |
| 2 tbsp | rice wine (optional) | 25 mL |

■ Place steak in freezer; freeze until firm but not frozen. Slice across the grain into 10 very thin slices; place in shallow dish. Combine soy sauce, 1 tbsp (15 mL) of the oil, sugar, vinegar and water; pour over steak. Cover and refrigerate for at least 2 hours or overnight.

■ Remove meat from marinade, reserving marinade. Roll each slice lengthwise around 1 onion, trimming onions to fit; secure with toothpicks.

■ In large heavy skillet, heat remaining oil over medium-high heat; cook meat rolls for 1 to 2 minutes, turning often, or until browned all over. Remove rolls and keep warm.

■ Add reserved marinade, and rice wine (if using), to skillet; cook for about 2 minutes or until reduced to 3 tbsp (50 mL). Remove toothpicks from rolls. Return rolls to pan; cook over medium heat for 1 to 2 minutes or until glazed, turning often. To serve, cut each roll into 1-inch (2.5 cm) pieces. Makes about 48 appetizers.

# Crispy Almond Mix

*This easy-to-make snack is so good it will disappear in no time. You can substitute dry-roasted unsalted peanuts for the almonds.*

| | | |
|---|---|---|
| 1 | egg white | 1 |
| 1 tsp | water | 5 mL |
| 2 cups | almonds (shelled but not blanched) | 500 mL |
| 2 cups | Shreddies cereal | 500 mL |
| 1/3 cup | granulated sugar | 75 mL |
| 1 tsp | cinnamon | 5 mL |
| 1 tsp | paprika | 5 mL |
| 1/4 tsp | chili powder | 1 mL |

■ In bowl, beat egg white with water until frothy. Add almonds and Shreddies; stir to coat.

■ Stir together sugar, cinnamon, paprika and chili powder; add to nut mixture and toss to coat well. Spread in well-greased 13- × 9-inch (3.5 L) baking dish. Bake in 250°F (120°C) oven for 1 hour, stirring every 15 minutes. Makes 4 cups (1 L).

# Marinated Goat Cheese Spread

*Marinated in olive oil and herbs, goat cheese, or chèvre, is delicious with French bread. Add more cheese, herbs and oil as needed to the jar and keep this appetizer on hand in the refrigerator at all times. Buy a cheese with a texture like firm cream cheese. If unavailable, you can substitute ricotta cheese.*

| | | |
|---|---|---|
| 1 lb | goat cheese | 500 g |
| 1/2 cup | chopped black olives | 125 mL |
| 1 tbsp | dried rosemary | 15 mL |
| 1 tbsp | whole black peppercorns | 15 mL |
| 2 | shallots, chopped | 2 |
| 2 | cloves garlic, crushed | 2 |
| | Extra-virgin olive oil | |
| | French bread | |

■ Cut cheese into large cubes; place in large jar. Add olives, rosemary, peppercorns, shallots and garlic. Add enough olive oil to cover. Refrigerate for at least 2 days.

■ To serve, remove garlic; spoon cheese, some of the herbs, olives and oil into serving bowl. Serve with bread. Makes 8 to 12 servings.

# Corned Beef Appetizer Balls

*This nippy spread is perfect with crackers or pumpernickel bread.*

| | | |
|---|---|---|
| 1 cup | shredded Cheddar cheese (about 4 oz/125 g) | 250 mL |
| 4 oz | cream cheese | 125 g |
| 6 oz | corned beef, shredded | 175 g |
| 1/4 cup | sweet pickle relish | 50 mL |
| 2 tsp | horseradish | 10 mL |
| 1 tsp | Dijon mustard | 5 mL |
| 1 tsp | Worcestershire sauce | 5 mL |
| 1/4 tsp | grated lemon rind | 1 mL |
| 1 tbsp | lemon juice | 15 mL |
| 1/2 cup | chopped fresh parsley | 125 mL |

■ In mixing bowl or food processor, beat together Cheddar and cream cheeses, corned beef, relish, horseradish, mustard, Worcestershire, lemon rind and lemon juice. Cover and refrigerate for 1 hour or until firm.

■ Shape corned beef mixture into 2 balls. *(Balls can be prepared to this point, wrapped and frozen. Thaw before continuing with recipe.)* To serve, roll each ball in parsley. Makes 8 to 10 servings.

# Smoked Salmon Flower Open-Faced Sandwiches

*These are easier to make than you think, and they look fabulous.*

| | | |
|---|---|---|
| 1/2 cup | unsalted butter | 125 mL |
| 2 tbsp | mayonnaise | 25 mL |
| 1 tbsp | Dijon mustard | 15 mL |
| 16 | squares (2 inches/5 cm) pumpernickel bread | 16 |
| 1 lb | smoked salmon, thinly sliced | 500 g |
| 16 | sprigs fresh parsley | 16 |

■ Combine butter, mayonnaise and mustard; spread over pumpernickel. Cut salmon into thirty-two 4- × 1-1/2-inch (10 × 4 cm) strips. Roll up 1 strip into tight curl.

■ Roll second strip around curl to form outside flower. Repeat with remaining strips. Place on pumpernickel; garnish with parsley sprig. Makes 16 appetizers.

# Almond-Turkey Roll

*This can also be served in a shallow bowl and covered with a thin layer of chutney. Serve with crackers.*

| | | |
|---|---|---|
| 1 lb | cream cheese | 500 g |
| 1 tsp | Worcestershire sauce | 5 mL |
| 1/2 tsp | curry powder | 2 mL |
| 1-1/2 cups | finely chopped cooked turkey | 375 mL |
| 1/3 cup | minced celery | 75 mL |
| 1/4 cup | minced fresh parsley | 50 mL |
| 1 cup | chopped toasted almonds* | 250 mL |

■ In food processor or mixing bowl, beat together cream cheese, Worcestershire sauce and curry powder until smooth. Stir in turkey, celery and parsley; cover and refrigerate until firm. Shape into 9-inch (23 cm) log; roll in almonds. Makes about 3 cups (750 mL).
*To toast almonds, bake on baking sheet in 350°F (180°C) oven for about 5 minutes or until golden.

# Creamy Pistachio-Salmon Pâté

*When entertaining, serve this pâté surrounded with rice crackers and French bread. Or pipe it onto Belgian endive leaves, into little choux puffs or hard-cooked egg white halves. If possible, use extra-smooth ricotta and drain if necessary.*

| | | |
|---|---|---|
| 1 | can (7-1/2 oz/213 g) sockeye salmon | 1 |
| 2 tbsp | lemon juice | 25 mL |
| 1/4 tsp | dried dillweed | 1 mL |
| 1/4 tsp | pepper | 1 mL |
| 1/2 lb | fresh ricotta cheese | 250 g |
| 2 | hard-cooked eggs | 2 |
| 1/4 cup | coarsely chopped pistachio nuts | 50 mL |
| | Salt | |

■ Drain salmon and remove bones. In food processor or blender, process salmon, lemon juice, dillweed and pepper until well blended.

■ Add cheese and eggs; process until puréed. Stir in nuts. Season with salt to taste. Spoon into serving bowl or crock. Cover and refrigerate for up to 3 days. Makes about 2-1/2 cups (625 mL).

# Shrimp and Feta Pizza Strips

*These easy pizza strips are especially light because they're made with flaky puff pastry instead of heavier bread dough. Serve after a game of bridge or an evening at the theatre.*

| | | |
|---|---|---|
| 1 | pkg (14 oz/397 g) frozen puff pastry, thawed | 1 |
| 1 cup | shredded mozzarella cheese | 250 mL |
| 1 | can (7-1/2 oz/213 mL) tomato sauce | 1 |
| 1 tsp | dried oregano | 5 mL |
| 1/4 lb | small shrimp | 125 g |
| 3 oz | feta cheese | 75 g |
| 1/4 tsp | dried dillweed | 1 mL |
| 2 tbsp | olive oil | 25 mL |

■ On lightly floured surface, roll out pastry to 16- × 11-inch (40 × 28 cm) rectangle. Cut into four 11- × 4-inch (28 × 10 cm) strips. Place on baking sheets and crimp up edges slightly. Sprinkle with mozzarella cheese; spread tomato sauce on top. Sprinkle with oregano; arrange shrimp on top of sauce.

■ Rinse feta under cold water and drain well; pat dry and crumble over pizza. Sprinkle with dillweed; drizzle with oil. Bake in 350°F (180°C) oven for about 35 minutes or until puffed and golden brown. Cut strips crosswise into 1-inch (2.5 cm) pieces. Serve hot. Makes about 8 servings.

# Credits

Recipes in THE CANADIAN LIVING COOKING COLLECTION have been created by the *Canadian Living* Test Kitchen and by the following food writers from across Canada: **Elizabeth Baird, Karen Brown, Joanna Burkhard, James Chatto, Diane Clement, David Cohlmeyer, Pam Collacott, Bonnie Baker Cowan, Pierre Dubrulle, Eileen Dwillies, Nancy Enright, Carol Ferguson, Margaret Fraser, Susan Furlan, Anita Goldberg, Barb Holland, Patricia Jamieson, Arlene Lappin, Anne Lindsay, Lispeth Lodge, Mary McGrath, Susan Mendelson, Bernard Meyer, Beth Moffatt, Rose Murray, Iris Raven, Gerry Shikatani, Jill Snider, Kay Spicer, Linda Stephen, Bonnie Stern, Lucy Waverman, Carol White, Ted Whittaker** and **Cynny Willet.**

The full-color photographs throughout are by Canada's leading food photographers, including **Fred Bird, Doug Bradshaw, Christopher Campbell, Nino D'Angelo, Frank Grant, Michael Kohn, Suzanne McCormick, Claude Noel, John Stephens** and **Mike Visser.**

**Editorial and Production Staff**: Hugh Brewster, Susan Barrable, Catherine Fraccaro, Wanda Nowakowska, Sandra L. Hall, Beverley Renahan and Bernice Eisenstein.

# Index

# LOOK FOR THESE BESTSELLING COOKBOOKS FROM *CANADIAN LIVING*

## The most trusted name in Canadian cooking